Booo! It's Halloween

# The Haunted History of Halloween (Spooktacular Tales and Traditions)

Blair Norman

Copyright@ Blair Norman 2022
All Rights Reserved

# TABLE OF CONTENTS

Introduction

Chapter 1: Ancient Origins of Halloween
– All Saints' Day
– Halloween Comes to America
– History of Trick-or-Treating
– Halloween Parties
– Halloween Movies
– All Souls Day and Soul Cakes
– Black Cats and Ghosts on Halloween
– Halloween Matchmaking and Lesser-Known Rituals

Chapter 2: History of Halloween
– Christian Origins and Historic Costumes
– Symbols
– Costumes
– Games and other activities
– Haunted Attractions
– Food
– Analogous Celebrations and Perspectives (Judaism, Islam, Hinduism, Neopaganism)
– Geography of Halloween

Chapter 3: Facts About Halloween
– 25 Interesting Halloween Facts
– 15 Halloween Trivia To Test Your Spooky Knowledge

# INTRODUCTION

Halloween is a holiday that is shortened to All Hallows' Eve and is celebrated on October 31, the night before All Saints' Day (also known as All Hallows' Day). The celebration begins three days before the Western Christian feast of All Saints and marks the beginning of the Halloween season, which culminates in All Souls' Day. Halloween is mostly celebrated non-religiously in most of Europe and North America. Halloween is observed on October 31, 2022, Monday.
The Celts of ancient Britain and Ireland's Samhain festival is where Halloween got its start. On modern calendars, it was believed that the new year would begin on November 1.

The day on which the herds were brought back from pasture and land tenures were renewed marked the beginning of the winter season. The spirits of those who had passed away were said to travel to the other world during the Samhain festival and to return to their homes during the year. To frighten away evil spirits and relight their hearth fires before the winter, people would light bonfires on hilltops. They would also sometimes wear masks or other disguises to avoid being recognized by the supposed ghosts. Beings like witches, hobgoblins, fairies, and demons came to be associated with the day in those ways. Additionally, it was believed that the time was favorable for marriage, health, and death divination. Feralia, a festival to honor the passing of the dead, and Pomona, a festival to honor the goddess of the harvest, were added by the Romans when they conquered the Celts in the first century CE.

All Saints' Day was first celebrated on May 13 in the 7th century CE by Pope Boniface IV. In the following century, it was moved to November 1, possibly to replace the pagan holiday with a Christian one. Halloween was born as a holy, or hallowed, night before All Saints' Day. The secular and sacred days had merged by the end of the Middle Ages. The Protestant holiday was basically abolished after the Reformation, but Halloween continued to be a secular holiday, especially in Britain. In the early American colonies, Halloween celebrations were generally outlawed. However, in the 1800s, festivals that celebrated the harvest and included Halloween elements were established. Beginning in the middle of the 19th century, a large number of immigrants, including Irish immigrants, came to the United States. They brought their Halloween traditions with them, and by the 20th century, Halloween had become one of the most important holidays in the United States, especially among children.

Halloween has come to be associated with several activities as a secular holiday. One is playing pranks, which are typically harmless. Celebrities dress in masks and costumes for parties and trick-or-treating, which is thought to have originated from the British custom of "soul cakes," which allowed the poor to beg for food. People who go trick-or-treating go from house to house threatening to pull a trick if they don't get a treat, usually candy. Bobbing for apples is a common game at Halloween parties, and it may have its origins in the Roman festival of Pomona. The holiday has included terrifying beings like vampires, witches, and skeletons in addition to black cats and skeletons. The jack-o'-lantern, which is actually a hollowed-out turnip that has been carved into a demon's face and lit by a candle inside, is another symbol. The United Nations Children's Fund (UNICEF) has attempted to incorporate fundraising for its programs into Halloween since the middle of the 20th century.

Why do we celebrate Halloween on October 31? What is the true history of Halloween?

From All Hallows' Eve, the word "Halloween" means "hallowed evening." Halloween originated as a pagan festival known as Samhain. Halloween costumes and trick-or-treating date back hundreds of years to people dressing up as saints and going door to door.

It's time to decorate your porch with pumpkins, start carving, and start thinking about Halloween treats and costumes as the leaves turn orange and yellow and the temperature drops. Halloween party games and terrifying fun are just around the corner for trick-or-treating, which may be more exciting for adults than trick-or-treating alone. Do you ever ponder the origins and history of Halloween amid all the festivities? We have answers for you regarding its significance, origin, and connection to a pagan holiday. The witches and wizards who are celebrated today are also a part of the story of the holiday, which began many, many years ago.

Of course, Halloween is always on the last Saturday in October, but before it got its current name, it was known as All Hallows' Eve and honored "hallows," also known as saints, just like All Saints' Day, which is celebrated on November 1 each year. Before the 7th century CE, All Hallow's Eve actually fell on May 13; however, Pope Boniface IV decided to move it to autumn, possibly to coincide with a religious celebration. As we know it today, the triple word "All Hallows' Eve" was eventually changed to "Halloween."

Why is Halloween celebrated on October 31?

Because the ancient Gaelic festival of Samhain, which is considered to be the earliest known origin of Halloween, took place on this day, Halloween falls on October 31. Observers believed that the boundary between this world and the next world became especially thin at this time, allowing them to connect with the dead and that it marked a pivotal time of year when the seasons changed. Some other cultures hold this belief; The Jewish holiday of Yom Kippur, which is also celebrated in October and involves praying for the dead, is associated with a similar concept. Additionally, this is where Halloween acquires the term "haunted."

The Origins of Halloween Activities
The Celts were polytheistic, so the early pagan holiday of Samhain included numerous rituals to connect with spirits. Although there isn't much information available about these celebrations, many people believe that the Celts dressed in animal hides to protect themselves from ghosts, enjoyed special feasts, and made lanterns by hollowing out gourds—hence the origin of jack-o-lanterns. The fundamental customs of the holiday remained ingrained in popular culture each year even after Christianity took control and the holiday's pagan undertones diminished over time; They only changed and became more advanced.

In earlier times, mystical rituals gave way to more lighthearted games and entertainment. For instance, the more lighthearted idea of telling the future took the place of the somewhat serious idea of connecting with the dead. On All Hallows' Eve, for instance, bobbing for apples became a popular game for divination: All of a woman's suitors would be chosen as apples, and the one she ended up biting into would supposedly be her future husband. In fact, in the 19th century, Halloween offered young women a huge, if somewhat spooky, opportunity to meet men.

The practice of looking in the mirror in the hopes of seeing a glimpse of the future was another well-liked All Hallows' Eve custom. Additionally, there are reports that fortune-cookie-like favors were distributed in the past. Messages were written on milk-soaked pieces of paper and folded before being stuffed into walnut shells. The milk would brown just enough on the shells as they were heated over a fire, allowing the message to magically appear on the paper for the recipient.

History of Halloween Costumes and Trick-or-Treating
Numerous people were said to dress as saints and go door to door singing or reciting verses. Additionally, children would go door to door in search of "soul cakes," a biscuit-like confection. A technical note:Soul cakes were originally celebrated on November 2 as part of All Souls' Day—yes, a third holiday! but as the idea developed into trick-or-treating, it eventually became a part of Halloween night. In the early to mid-1900s, the idea of giving candy to children in the hope that they would be immune to holiday pranks also became commonplace in the United States.

The costumes also changed over time. Even though they started as sincere tributes to saints, this custom probably went out of style at some point...until young Scottish and Irish pranksters came up with the idea to dress up in scary clothes again to scare neighbors who weren't expecting it. Halloween costumes became simultaneously frightening, spooky, funny, and creative as a result of these local thugs.

How Halloween Is Celebrated Today
Although Halloween is still a well-known holiday in the United States, it almost didn't make it there. As a result of their disapproval of the pagan origins of the holiday, the Puritans did not participate in the festivities. However, the holiday returned to popular culture when a greater number of Irish and Scottish immigrants arrived in the United States. In the very first American colonial Halloween celebrations,

large public gatherings were held to commemorate the upcoming harvest, sing, dance, and tell ghost stories.

By the early 20th century, most people in North America (those who liked candy and wore costumes) probably celebrated Halloween. On October 31st, the only spooky spirits we'll be discussing are the witch and ghost costumes our friends are wearing, so once again, we'll all be enjoying our favorite candy and admiring the decorations of our neighbors.

Chapter 1

## ANCIENT ORIGINS OF HALLOWEEN

Halloween is an annual holiday that falls on October 31. In 2022, it will fall on Monday, October 31. The custom dates back to the ancient Celtic festival of Samhain, during which people wore costumes and lit bonfires to ward off ghosts. Pope Gregory III established November 1 as a day to honor all saints in the eighth century. Soon, some Samhain customs were incorporated into All Saints Day. All Hallows Eve was celebrated the night before, and later Halloween was celebrated. Halloween became a day filled with activities like trick-or-treating, carving jack-o-lanterns, festive gatherings, dressing up in costumes, and eating treats over time.

The Celtic festival of Samhain (pronounced sow-in) is where the origins of Halloween can be found. On November 1, the Celts, who lived 2,000 years ago, mostly in what is now Ireland, the UK, and northern France, celebrated the beginning of the new year. This day marked the end of the harvest and the beginning of the dark, cold winter, a time of year associated frequently with human death. The Celts believed that the night before the new year blurred the line between the living and dead worlds. It was believed that the spirits of the deceased returned to the earth, so they celebrated Samhain on October 31.

Celts believed that the presence of the otherworldly spirits made it simpler for the Druids or Celtic priests to make predictions, in addition to causing trouble and harming crops. These prophecies were an important source of comfort during the long, gloomy winter for people who were completely dependent on the volatile natural world. Druids constructed enormous sacred bonfires to commemorate the occasion, where people congregate to burn crops and animals as offerings to the Celtic gods. The Celts attempted to predict each other's futures while participating in the celebration by dressing in costumes that typically included animal skins and heads.

They're-lit their hearth fires from the sacred bonfire, which they had already put out earlier that evening after the celebration was over to help them survive the coming winter. Did you recognize it? Halloween accounts for one-quarter of all candy purchases made annually in the United States.

The Roman Empire had already conquered the majority of Celtic land by 43 A.D. During the 400 years that they ruled the Celtic lands, two Roman festivals were mixed in with the traditional Celtic Samhain festival. The first was Feralia, a Roman holiday observed toward the end of October to honor those who had passed away. The second day was dedicated to Pomona, a Roman goddess of trees and fruit. The apple is the symbol of Pomona, and the fact that this celebration is part of Samhain probably explains why people still bob for apples on Halloween.

Most Halloween costumes were made at home in the early 20th century and focused on spooky themes rather than current events. Early costumes were designed to conceal one's identity in a spooky manner that evoked themes like ghosts, witches, black cats, or the moon rather than dressing up as a particular creature or character.

**All Saints Day**
All Saints' Day was established in the Western church on May 13, 609 A.D., when Pope Boniface IV dedicated the Pantheon in Rome in honor of all Christian martyrs. Later, Pope Gregory III changed the date of the festival from May 13 to November 1 to include all martyrs

and saints. By the 9th century, Christianity had spread to Celtic lands, where it gradually replaced older Celtic rites and merged with them. The church established All Souls' Day on November 2 in 1000 A.D. as as a day to honor the deceased. Today, it is generally accepted that the church was attempting to substitute a related, church-approved holiday for the Celtic festival of the dead. Similar to Samhain, large bonfires, parades, and costumes as saints, angels, or demons were worn on All Souls' Day. The celebration of All Saints' Day was also known as All-Hallows or All-Hallowmas (from the Middle English word Alholowmesse, which means All Saints' Day), and the night before it, the Celtic festival of Samhain, began to be known as All-Hallows Eve, and eventually Halloween.

**Halloween Comes to America**
In colonial New England, due to the rigid Protestant belief systems there, Halloween celebrations were severely limited. Maryland and the southern colonies saw much more Halloween celebrations. A distinct American version of Halloween began to emerge as the beliefs and practices of various European ethnic groups and American Indians combined. "Play parties," which were open-to-the-public celebrations of the harvest, were among the initial celebrations. Neighbors would dance and sing, tell each other their fortunes, and tell stories about the dead.

Did you know? Costumes for pets are being purchased by more people. In 2019, costumes for pets cost $490 million, more than double the amount spent in 2010. Ghost tales and all kinds of mischief were also part of the Colonial Halloween celebrations. Halloween was not yet a national holiday until the middle of the 19th century when annual autumn celebrations were common.

America received an influx of new immigrants during the second half of the nineteenth century. Halloween became more widely celebrated across the country thanks to these new immigrants, particularly the millions of Irish people who fled the Irish Potato Famine.

**History of Trick-or-Treating**
Americans began dressing up in costumes and going house to house asking for food or money after borrowing ideas from European cultures. This eventually led to the "trick-or-treat" tradition that we know today. Using mirrors, apple parings, or yarn, young women believed they could predict their future husbands' names or appearances on Halloween.

At the end of the 1800s, there was a push in the United States to make Halloween a holiday more about getting together with friends and neighbors than about ghosts, tricks, and witchcraft. Halloween parties for adults and kids became the most popular way to celebrate the holiday at the turn of the century. Games, seasonal foods, and festive costumes were the main attractions at parties.

Newspapers and community leaders advised parents to eliminate anything "frightening" or "grotesque" from Halloween festivities. By the turn of the twentieth century, the majority of Halloween's religious and superstitious undertones had vanished as a result of these efforts.

**Halloween Parties**
By the 1920s and 1930s, Halloween had evolved into a secular but community-focused holiday, with town-wide Halloween parties and parades serving as the main forms of entertainment. During this time, vandalism began to plague some celebrations in many communities, despite the best efforts of many schools and communities. By the 1950s, town leaders had managed to control vandalism, and

Halloween had become primarily a holiday for young people. Parties moved away from town civic centers and into classrooms or homes because of the high number of young children during the baby boom of the 1950s.

The centuries-old tradition of trick-or-treating was also revived between 1920 and 1950. A low-cost way for the entire community to celebrate Halloween was through trick-or-treating. In theory, families could also prevent children in their neighborhood from being tricked by giving them small treats. As a result, a brand-new custom was developed in the United States. Halloween is the country's second-largest commercial holiday, after Christmas, with an estimated $6 billion in annual spending by Americans.

**Halloween Movies**
Scary Halloween movies have a long history of being box office hits, which brings us back to the topic of commercial success. The "Halloween" franchise is based on the 1978 original film directed by John Carpenter and starring Donald Pleasance, Nick Castle, Jamie Lee Curtis, and Tony Moran. Other classic Halloween movies include the "Halloween" series. In the movie "Halloween," a young boy named Michael Myers kills his 17-year-old sister and is sentenced to prison. However, on Halloween night, he eludes as a teen and goes in search of his old home and a new target. Jamie Lee Curtis and Nick Castle starred in a 2018 direct sequel to the original "Halloween." In 2021, the twelfth film in the "Halloween" series was released as a sequel titled "Halloween Kills."

Scream, Nightmare on Elm Street, and Friday the 13 were all influenced by "Halloween," which is considered a classic horror film due to its creepy soundtrack. Halloween films like "Hocus Pocus," "The Nightmare Before Christmas," "Beetlejuice," and "It's the Great

Pumpkin, Charlie Brown" are more suitable for families. Nosferatu, a German film from 1922:A Symphony of Horror is a fake version of Bram Stoker's Dracula, which was published in 1897. Even before Bram Stoker's novel, there have been tales of undead creatures consuming the living.

**All Souls Day and Soul Cakes**
The American Halloween custom of trick-or-treating probably originates from the early All Souls' Day parades held in England. During the festivities, poor people would beg for food, and families would give them pastries known as "soul cakes" in exchange for their promise to pray for the dead relatives of the family.

The church encouraged the distribution of soul cakes as a replacement for the traditional practice of offering food and wine to wandering spirits. Children eventually adopted the practice, which was referred to as "going a-souling," in which they were given money, food, and ale for visiting the homes in their neighborhood. Halloween's costume-wearing custom has Celtic as well as European roots. Winter was a frightening and uncertain season hundreds of years ago. The short days of winter were filled with constant worry for many people who were afraid of the dark and ran out of food frequently. People believed they would encounter ghosts if they left their homes on Halloween when it was believed that ghosts returned to the real world. People would wear masks when they left their homes after dark so that the ghosts would mistake them for other spirits. This was done to avoid being seen by the ghosts. People would leave bowls of food outside their homes on Halloween to appease the ghosts and deter them from entering. This was done to keep the ghosts away from their homes.

Throughout history, images of witches have taken a variety of forms, ranging from evil, wart-nosed women huddled over a boiling pot to hag-faced, wailing beings riding through the sky on brooms with pointy hats. Vampires are evil, mythological beings that roam the night in search of victims in exchange for their blood. However, the actual history of witches is dark and goes back as far as approximately 900 B.C.Vampires have a long history that predates Bram Stoker, even though they are frequently associated with Count Dracula, the legendary character in his epic 1897 novel Dracula. These sinister characters represent a superstition that flourished in the Middle Ages and is reminiscent of Greek mythology.

**Black Cats and Ghosts on Halloween**
This has always been a holiday full of magic, mystery, and superstition. It all started as a Celtic celebration of the summer's end during which people felt especially close to friends and family who had passed away. To assist loved ones in returning to the spirit world, these friendly spirits placed places at the dinner table, left treats on doorsteps and along the roadside, and lit candles.

Halloween ghosts of today are frequently depicted as more terrifying and evil, and our traditions and superstitions are also scarier. We avoid encountering black cats out of concern that they might bring us bad luck. This notion dates back to the Middle Ages when many people held the belief that witches could evade detection by transforming into black cats.

For the same reason, we try not to walk underneath ladders. This superstition may have originated from the ancient Egyptians, who held the belief that triangles were sacred. It may also have something to do with the fact that walking under a ladder that is leaning can be quite dangerous. We also try to avoid spilling salt, stepping on road cracks, or breaking mirrors, especially around Halloween.

**Halloween Matchmaking and Lesser-Known Rituals**
However, what about the Halloween customs and beliefs that modern trick-or-treaters have completely forgotten? Numerous of these outmoded rituals emphasized the living over the dead and the future over the past. In particular, many of them involved assisting young women in locating their potential husbands and reassuring them that they would eventually wed—hopefully by Halloween next year. On Halloween night in 18th-century Ireland, a matchmaking cook might bury a ring in her mashed potatoes in the hope that the diner who found it would find true love.

A suitable young woman in Scotland was advised by fortune tellers to name a hazelnut for each of her suitors and then toss the nuts into the fireplace. According to the tale, the nut's ashes instead of popping or exploding represented the girl's future husband. The reverse was true in some versions of this legend:A love that would not endure was symbolized by the nut that burned away.)A different legend stated that a young woman would have a dream about her future husband if she consumed a sweet mixture of walnuts, hazelnuts, and nutmeg before going to bed on Halloween.

In the hope that the apple peels would fall to the ground in the form of their future husbands' initials, young women threw them over their shoulders; stood in front of mirrors in darkened rooms while holding candles and looking over their shoulders for their husbands' faces, and tried to learn about their futures by looking at egg yolks floating in a bowl of water.

The competition was stronger at other rituals. At some Halloween parties, the first person to wed would be the person who found a burr on a chestnut hunt. On other occasions, the first apple bobber to be successful would be the first down the aisle. Obviously, these Halloween superstitions rely on the goodwill of the very same "spirits" whose presence the early Celts so keenly felt, whether we're seeking romantic advice or trying to avoid seven years of bad luck.

# Chapter 2

## HISTORY OF HALLOWEEN

*Christian Origins and Historic Customs*

History and customs from the Christian era Halloween are thought to have its origins in Christian beliefs and practices." All Hallows' Eve," which occurs the night before the Christian holy days of All Hallows' Day (also known as All Saints' Day) on November 1 and All Souls' Day on November 2, is where the English word "Halloween" comes from. Christmas, Easter, and Pentecost, as well as the All Hallows' Day celebration, have had vigils that began the night before since the time of the early Church. Western Christians observe these three days, which are collectively referred to as Allhallowtide, as a time to honor all saints and pray for those whose souls have recently passed away and have not yet reached Heaven. Several churches held commemorations of all saints and martyrs on various dates, mostly in the spring. It was held on May 13 in Roman Edessa in the fourth century, and Pope Boniface IV re-dedicated the Pantheon in Rome to "St. Mary and all martyrs" on May 13 in 609. Lemuria, an ancient Roman festival honoring the dead, fell on this day.

In the years 731–741, Pope Gregory III built an oratory in St. Peter's in the eighth century to house the relics "of the holy apostles and all saints, martyrs, and confessors."It may have been dedicated on November 1, according to some sources, or it may have been on Palm Sunday in April 732. There is evidence that churches in Ireland and Northumbria held a feast on November 1 to honor all the saints by 800. It's possible that Alcuin of Northumbria, a member of Charlemagne's court, introduced this date in the Frankish Empire on November 1st.In the Frankish Empire, it became the official date in 835. Although it is claimed that both Germanic-speaking and

Celtic-speaking peoples commemorated the dead at the beginning of winter, others assert that this was a Germanic concept, while others assert that it was influenced by Celtic culture. Because it is a natural time of "dying," they may have thought it was the best time to do so. Additionally, it is suggested that the change was made on the "practical grounds that Rome in summer could not accommodate the great number of pilgrims who flocked to it" and possibly due to public health concerns regarding Roman Fever, which killed several people in Rome's hot summers.

By the end of the 12th century, they had evolved into holy days of obligation in Western Christianity and included customs like ringing church bells in memory of souls in hell.``Customary for criers dressed in black to parade the streets, ringing a bell of mournful sound and calling on all good Christians to remember the poor souls" was another thing that took place. It has been suggested that trick-or-treating originated with the tradition of baking and sharing soul cakes for all christened souls during Halloween. The practice has been practiced in parts of England, Wales, Flanders, Bavaria, and Austria since at least the 15th century. During Allhalloween, poor groups, most of whom were children, would go door to door collecting soul cakes in exchange for praying for the deceased, particularly their friends and family. The term for this was "souling."In addition, soul cakes were made available to the souls themselves or to the "souls" who would serve as their representatives. Soul cakes were frequently emblazoned with a cross, similar to the Lenten custom of hot cross buns, indicating that they were made for charity. In his comedy The Two Gentlemen of Verona (1593), Shakespeare mentions souling. Christians carried "lanterns made of hollowed-out turnips" that may have originally represented the souls of the deceased while souling; The purpose of jack-o-lanterns was to ward off evil spirits. During the 19th century, homes in Ireland, Flanders, Bavaria, and Tyrol lit candles on All Saints' and All Souls' Day. These candles were referred to as "soul lights" because they "guided the souls back to visit their earthly homes." On All Souls' Day, graveside candles were also lit in many of these locations. In Brittany, relatives' graves were given milk-based libations, or food was left on the dinner table overnight for those who came back; a tradition also prevalent in Tyrol and a portion of Italy.

Prince Sorie Conteh, a Christian minister, made the connection between the belief in vengeful ghosts and the wearing of costumes: Traditionally, it was believed that the deceased wandered the earth up until All Saints' Day, and All Hallows' Eve provided the deceased with one last opportunity to exact revenge on their foes before departing for the next world. People would don masks or costumes to avoid being recognized by any soul who might be seeking such vengeance. During the Middle Ages, churches in Europe that were unable to display the relics of martyred saints at Allhalloween allowed parishioners to dress as saints instead because they were too poor to do so. This custom is still observed by some Christians on Halloween today. This may have been a Christianization of an earlier pagan practice, according to Lesley Bannatyne." That once a year, on Hallowe'en, the dead of the churchyards rose for one wild, hideous carnival known as the danse macabre, which was often depicted in church decoration," was a belief held by many Christians on the continent of Europe, particularly in France. In their book The New Cambridge Medieval History, Christopher Allmand and Rosamond McKitterick claim that the danse macabre advised Christians "not to forget the end of all earthly things." People "dressing up as corpses from various strata of society" performed the danse macabre at European village pageants and court masques, which may have been the origin of Halloween costume parties.

During the Reformation, Protestants in Britain attacked these practices, calling purgatory a "popish" belief that was incompatible with the Calvinist doctrine of predestination. During the Elizabethan reform, state-sanctioned ceremonies for praying for souls in purgatory and interceding for saints were banned. However, All Hallows Day was still included in the English liturgical calendar to "commemorate saints as godly human beings."The theology of All Hallows' Eve was redefined for some Nonconformist Protestants; Catholics frequently assert that souls cannot be traveling from Purgatory to Heaven. Instead, it is believed that the so-called ghosts are in fact evil spirits."Hades, or the Bosom of Abraham, was a secondary state that was held by other Protestants. Catholics and Protestants continued souling, candlelit procession, and church bell ringing for the dead in some areas; This bell-ringing was eventually stopped by the Anglican church." Barns and homes were blessed to protect people and livestock from the effect of witches, who were believed to accompany the malignant spirits as they traveled the earth," write professor of medieval archaeology Mark Donnelly and historian Daniel Diehl. Guy Fawkes Night, which took some of England's traditions with it on November 5th, took the place of Hallowtide in England after 1605. New, unofficial Hallowe'en traditions emerged in England as the official celebrations of saints' intercession came to an end. On All Hallows' Eve, Catholic families gathered on hills in rural Lancashire between the 18th and 19th centuries. While the others kneeled around him and prayed for the souls of relatives and friends until the flames went out, one man held a bunch of burning straw on a pitchfork. Teen lay was the term for this. Hertfordshire followed a similar tradition, and Derbyshire lit "tindle" fires. Some people suggested that the original purpose of these "tindles" was to "guide the poor souls back to earth."Because they "were important to the life cycle and rites of passage of local communities," they were not suppressed in Scotland and Ireland because it would have been difficult to curb them.

Additionally, the old Allhallowtide customs were in direct opposition to Reformed teaching.

Before going to church, families in some parts of Italy up until the 15th century served a meal to relatives' ghosts. On All Hallows' Day in Italy in the nineteenth century, churches staged "theatrical re-enactments of scenes from the lives of the saints," with "participants represented by realistic wax figures."In the year 1823, the graveyard of Holy Spirit Hospital in Rome featured a scene in which the bodies of people who had recently passed away were arranged around a wax statue of an angel that was pointing toward heaven.``Parish priests went house to house, asking for small gifts of food which they shared among themselves throughout that night" was the custom in the same nation. They continue to bake special pastries in Spain that are known as "bones of the holy" (Spanish:Huesos de Santo) and buried them there. During Halloween, Christian processions and services are led by priests at cemeteries in Spain, France, and Latin America. After the services, people stay awake all night. A procession to the city cemetery on All Halloween in 19th-century San Sebastián attracted beggars who "appeal[ed] to the tender recollections of one's deceased relatives and friends ' for sympathy.

*Influence from Gaelic folk*
An Irish Halloween mask from the early 20th century on display at the Museum of Country Life Today's Halloween traditions are thought to have been influenced by folk beliefs and practices from Celtic-speaking nations, some of which are thought to have pagan roots."There was throughout Ireland an uneasy truce existing between customs and beliefs associated with Christianity and those associated with religions that were Irish before Christianity arrived," according to a folklorist named Jack Santino. The Gaelic festival of Samhain is frequently linked to the origins of Halloween customs.

In Ireland, Scotland, and the Isle of Man, Samhain is one of the quarter days on the medieval Gaelic calendar. Between October 31 and November 1 is when it is observed. The Brythonic Celts celebrated a similar festival, Calan Gaeaf in Wales, Kalan Gwav in Cornwall, and Kalan Goav in Brittany; a name that translates to "the first day of winter."The Celts defined sunset as the end and beginning of the day. Thus, according to contemporary estimation, the festival began the evening before November 1. In some of the earliest works of Irish literature, Samhain is mentioned. Up until the 19th century, historians used these names to refer to Celtic Halloween costumes, and they are still the Gaelic and Welsh names for Halloween.

Samhain was a festival that marked the end of harvest and the beginning of winter, also known as the "darker half of the year."The transition from this world to the Otherworld was seen as a liminal period. This meant that the Aos S, also known as "fairies" or "spirits," could enter this world more easily and were particularly active."Degraded versions of ancient gods [...] whose power remained active in the people's minds even after they had been officially replaced by later religious beliefs," according to the majority of scholars. They were feared and respected, and when people came close to their homes, they frequently invoked God's protection. To ensure that both people and livestock would survive the winter, the Aos S were placated at Samhain. They received portions of the crops or food and drink offerings left outside. It was also said that the spirits of the deceased returned to their homes in search of hospitality. To welcome them, seating arrangements were made at the dinner table and by the fire. In many cultures, the notion that the spirits of the deceased must be purged when they return home on a single night of the year appears to have ancient roots."Candles would be lit and formally offered prayers for the souls of the dead in 19th century Ireland."After this, games, eating, and drinking would begin.

Household celebrations in Ireland and Britain, particularly in the Celtic-speaking regions, included divination games and rituals that were intended to foretell one's future, particularly regarding marriage and death. Apple bobbing, nut roasting, scrying or mirror-gazing, pouring molten lead or egg whites into water, dream interpretation, and other customs made use of apples and nuts. Some rituals involved lighting special bonfires. It was believed that their smoke, flames, and ashes had cleansing and protective properties. To protect homes and fields, bonfire-lit torches were sometimes carried around in the sun. The fires are said to have been some kind of sympathetic or imitative magic because they mimicked the Sun and prevented winter's decay and darkness. Additionally, they were used for divination and protection from evil spirits. In some parishes in Scotland, the church elders outlawed these bonfires and divination games. In order to "prevent the souls of the dead from falling to earth," bonfires were also lit in Wales. These bonfires later "kept the devil away."

In Ireland, Scotland, the Isle of Man, and Wales, the festival included mumming and guise since at least the 16th century. This involved reciting verses or songs in exchange for food while going house to house in costume (or disguise). It's possible that, similar to "souling," it was once a custom in which people impersonated the Aos S, or the dead souls, and received offerings on their behalf. It was also believed that assuming the form of these beings or concealing oneself from them would protect oneself. A hobby horse was one of the guisers in some areas of southern Ireland. In exchange for food, young people were led from house to house by a man dressed as a Láir Bhán (white mare). Some of the verses had pagan undertones. The "Muck Olla " might grant the household good fortune if they gave food; Failure to do so would result in misfortune. With blackened, painted, or masked faces, young people in Scotland would travel from house to house, frequently threatening to cause trouble if they were not welcomed. According to F. Marian McNeill, the ancient festival featured people dressed as spirits and had their faces blackened or marked with ashes from the sacred bonfire. In some parts of Wales, men dressed as gwrachod, terrifying creatures. Cross-dressing was popular among young people in Glamorgan and Orkney in the late 19th and early 20th centuries.

Mumming was part of other festivals in other parts of Europe, but it was "especially appropriate to a night upon which supernatural beings were said to be abroad and could be imitated or warded off by human wanderers" in the Celtic-speaking regions. In Ireland and the Scottish Highlands, pranks were played by "imitating malignant spirits" at least since the 18th century. Halloween pranks and costumes did not become popular in England until the 20th century. Pranksters made lanterns out of hollowed-out turnips or mangel wurzels, which were frequently carved with horrifying faces. The people who made the lanterns believed that they were either used to ward off evil spirits or that they represented the spirits. In the 19th century, they were prevalent in Somerset as well as a portion of Ireland and the Scottish Highlands (see Punkie Night). They came to be known as jack-o-lanterns when they spread throughout other parts of Britain in the 20th century.

*Spread to North America*
According to Lesley Bannatyne and Cindy Ott, Anglican colonists in the southern United States and Catholic colonists in Maryland "recognized All Hallow's Eve in their church calendars," despite the Puritans of New England's strong opposition to the holiday and other

established Church-established celebrations, such as Christmas. Halloween was not widely celebrated in North America, at least not according to Almanacs from the late 18th and early 19th centuries.

Halloween didn't become a major holiday in the United States until the 19th century when a lot of Irish and Scottish people moved in. The Irish and Scots brought the majority of American Halloween customs, but "In Cajun areas, a nocturnal Mass was said in cemeteries on Halloween night."Families frequently spent the entire night at the graveside, lighting blessed candles on the graves. By the beginning of the 20th century, it was celebrated by people of all social, racial, and religious backgrounds from coast to coast. Initially confined to these immigrant communities, it gradually became a part of mainstream society. By the late 20th and early 21st centuries, these Halloween customs had spread to numerous other nations, including mainland Europe, thanks to American influence.

*Symbols*
At Halloween, yards, public areas, and some homes may be decorated with traditionally macabre symbols like skeletons, ghosts, cobwebs, gravestones, and witches that look scary.
The evolution of Halloween-related artifacts and symbols occurred over time. On All Hallows' Eve, guisers traditionally carry jack-o-lanterns to frighten evil spirits. The jack-o-lantern is associated with popular Irish Christian folklore, which says it represents a "soul who has been denied entry into both heaven and hell": Jack is tricked into climbing a tree by the Devil while driving home from a night of drinking. The cross is imprinted into the bark by a quick-thinking Jack, trapping the devil. Jack agrees that Satan will never be able to take his soul. Jack's death denies him entry into heaven after a life of lying, drinking, and sin. The Devil refuses to let Jack enter hell and hurls a lump of live coal straight at him, keeping his promise. Jack put the

coal in a turnip that had been hollowed out because it was cold. Since then, he and his lantern have been looking for a place to rest.

The turnip has traditionally been carved for Halloween in Ireland and Scotland. However, immigrants to North America used the native pumpkin, which is much softer and larger than a turnip, making it easier to carve. The American custom of carving pumpkins dates back to 1837 and was originally associated with harvest time in general. It wasn't until the middle to late 19th century that it became specifically associated with Halloween.

Christian eschatology, national customs, and Gothic and horror literature (such as the novels Frankenstein;) are just a few of the many influences that have contributed to the modern Halloween imagery. or, Dracula and The Modern Prometheus), as well as classic films about horror like Frankenstein (1931) and The Mummy (1932). As "a reminder of death and the transitory quality of human life," the image of the skull, which is a reference to Golgotha in the Christian tradition, can be found in memento mori and vanitas compositions; As a result, skulls are a common Halloween decoration that continues this theme." decorated with a depiction of the Last Judgment, complete with graves opening and the dead rising, with a heaven filled with angels and a hell filled with devils," is a tradition that has permeated this triduum. Scottish poet John Mayne wrote in 1780 about Halloween pranks, making it one of the earliest works on the subject. What terrifying pranks follow!", as well as the "Bogies" (ghosts) that were supernaturally associated with the night, which had an impact on Robert Burns' "Halloween" (1785). Pumpkins, corn husks, and scarecrows, all elements of autumn, are also common. Around Halloween, homes are frequently decorated with symbols of this kind. The themes of death, evil and mythical monsters are prevalent in Halloween imagery. Black cats, long associated with witches, are another common Halloween symbol. Halloween traditionally celebrates the colors black, orange, and occasionally purple.

*Trick or treating and Guising*
Trick-or-treating is a traditional Halloween celebration for children. Children pose the question, "Trick or treat?" as they move house to house in costume, asking for sweets like candy or even cash. A "threat" to cause harm to the homeowners or their property if no reward is given is implied by the word "trick."The medieval art of mumming, which is closely related to souling, is said to have inspired the practice. According to John Pymm's writing, "the Christian Church celebrated many of the feast days associated with the presentation of mumming plays."All Hallows' Eve, Christmas, Twelfth Night, and Shrove Tuesday were among these feast days. Mumming was a form of fancy dress masked individuals who "paraded the streets and entered houses to dance or play dice in silence" in Germany, Scandinavia, and other parts of Europe.

From the Middle Ages to the 1930s, people in England followed the Christian tradition of souling on Halloween. Soulers, both Protestant and Catholic, would go from parish to parish and beg the wealthy for soul cakes in exchange for praying for the souls of the people giving them and their friends. On All Hallows Eve, children in rural areas in the Philippines engage in the ritual of souling, known as Pangangaluluwa. People drape themselves in white cloths to represent souls and then visit houses, where they sing in return for prayers and sweets.

Guising, in which children wear costumes and go door to door in search of food or coins, is a common Halloween tradition in Scotland and Ireland. On Halloween in 1895, masqueraders dressed as turnips and carrying lanterns made of scooped-out turnips visited homes to be rewarded with cakes, fruit, and money. Until the 2000s, "Help the Halloween Party" was the most frequently chanted phrase among children in Ireland. In 1911, a newspaper in Kingston, Ontario, Canada, reported that children were "guising" around the neighborhood. This was the first mention of the Halloween tradition in North America.

The first American book-length history of Halloween was written by Massachusetts-based American historian and author Ruth Edna Kelley; The Book of Hallowe'en (1919), and references souling in the chapter "Hallowe'en in America".Kelley includes references to transatlantic customs in her book; They have been nurtured by Americans, who are making this a celebration comparable to what it must have been like when it was at its best overseas. In the United States, all Halloween traditions are directly or indirectly derived from those of other nations.

While the first reference to "guising" in North America occurs in 1911, another reference to ritual begging on Halloween appears, place unknown, in 1915, with a third reference in Chicago in 1920. In the Blackie Herald of Alberta, Canada, in 1927, the phrase "trick or treat" appears for the first time in print. Most of the thousands of Halloween postcards that were printed between the turn of the 20th century and the 1920s typically depict children but do not depict trick-or-treating. The term "trick-or-treating" first appeared in the United States in 1934 and was first used in a national publication in 1939. However, it does not appear that trick-or-treating became widespread in North America until the 1930s.

"Children are offered treats from the trunks of cars parked in a church parking lot" or "Halloween tailgating" is a well-known variation of trick-or-treating. Sometimes, trunk-or-treating also occurs in school parking lots. During a trunk-or-treat event, each car's trunk (or boot) is decorated with a particular theme, such as characters from children's literature, movies, the Bible, or job roles. The fact that it "solves the rural conundrum in which homes [are] built a half-mile apart" and that trunk-or-treating is perceived as being safer than going door-to-door appeals to parents as well as the fact that it has gained popularity.

*Costumes*
Costumes for Halloween were typically based on scary-looking witches, devils, vampires, ghosts, and skeletons. The selection of costumes grew over time to include fictional characters, celebrities, and common archetypes like ninjas and princesses.
By the late 19th century, Halloween celebrations in Scotland and Ireland included dressing up in costumes and "guising." A Scottish term, the tradition is called "guising" because of the disguises or costumes worn by the children. The masks are referred to as "false faces" in Ireland. In the early 20th century, when trick-or-treating became popular in Canada and the United States in the 1920s and 1930s, costume parties became increasingly popular in the United States, both for adults and children.

Eddie J. Smith presents a theological viewpoint in his book Halloween, Hallowed is Thy Name to the wearing of costumes on All Hallows' Eve, suggesting that by dressing up as creatures "who at one time caused us to fear and tremble", people can poke fun at Satan "whose kingdom has been plundered by our Saviour". Traditional memento mori decorations feature skeletons and dead people.
A fundraising campaign called "Trick-or-Treat for UNICEF" aims to support UNICEF, a United Nations program that aids children in developing nations. The program, which began as a local event in a Northeast Philadelphia neighborhood in 1950 and spread to the entire country in 1952, involves schools (or, more recently, corporate

sponsors like Hallmark at their licensed stores) handing out small boxes to trick-or-treaters so that they can solicit small change donations from the homes they visit. Since its inception, it is estimated that children have raised more than $118 million for UNICEF. In Canada, UNICEF decided in 2006 to end their Halloween collection boxes because of safety and administrative issues; Instead, they redesigned the program after consulting with schools.

In 1974, the New York Village Halloween Parade began to be held every year; It is the largest Halloween parade in the world and the only major nighttime parade in America. It attracts over 60,000 people in costumes, two million spectators, and a global television audience. In the United States, ethnic costume stereotypes have come under increasing scrutiny since the late 2010s. Public disapproval of such and other potentially offensive costumes is growing.

*Pet Costumes*
A National Retail Federation report from 2018 estimates that 30 million Americans will spend $480 million in 2018 on costumes for their pets for Halloween. This is significantly more than the estimated $200 million in 2010. The pumpkin, the hot dog, and the bumblebee are the most popular pet costumes. The bumblebee is third.

*Games and other activities*
Halloween is traditionally associated with several games. Some of these games started as rituals for divination or ways to predict one's future, especially when it comes to death, marriage, and children. Because they were regarded as "deadly serious" practices, these rituals were performed by a "rare few" in rural communities during the Middle Ages. These divination games have been "a common feature of the household festivities" in Ireland and Britain over the past few centuries. Hazelnuts and apples are common ingredients. Apples

were strongly associated with immortality and the Otherworld in Celtic mythology, whereas hazelnuts were associated with divine wisdom. They may also be derived from Roman celebrations of Pomona, according to some.

Between the 17th and 20th centuries, Halloween celebrations in Ireland and Britain typically included the following activities. Some have spread more widely and are still popular today. Apple bobbing or dunking, also known as "dooking" in Scotland, is a common game in which players must remove apples from a large basin or tub filled with water using only their teeth. Attempting to drive a fork into an apple while kneeling on a chair and holding it between your teeth is one variation of dunking. Scones coated in syrup or treacle are another common game that is played by stringing them up; While they are still attached to the string, these can only be eaten with your hands, which will inevitably result in a sticky face. Hanging a small wooden rod from the ceiling at head height with a lit candle on one end and an apple on the other was another popular game. Everyone takes turns using their teeth to try to catch the apple as the rod is turned around. In Ireland and Britain, foretelling one's future partner or spouse is one of the traditional activities. The peel would be tossed over the shoulder after an apple was peeled in one long strip. It is thought that the peel will land in the shape of the first letter of the name of the future spouse. A fire would be used to roast two hazelnuts; one is named after the roaster, and the other is named after the person they want. If the nuts run away from the heat, it's a bad sign; however, if they roast slowly, it means they'll go well together. Baked oatmeal bannock with salt would be used; The individual would consume it in three bites before going to bed without speaking or drinking. A dream in which their future spouse offers them a drink to quench their thirst is said to result from this. On Halloween night, unmarried women were told that if they sat in a darkened room and looked into a mirror, the face of their future husband would show up. The practice was so widespread that it was featured on greeting cards in the late 19th and early 20th centuries.

Picn, which translates to "blindfolds," was another well-liked game in Ireland. A person would select one of several saucers after being blindfolded. The item in the saucer might tell them something about the future:A ring would indicate their impending union; clay, that they would pass away quickly, possibly within a year; water so they could leave; rosary beads in the hopes that they would obtain Holy Orders (such as becoming nuns, priests, or monks); a coin, ensuring their prosperity; a bean, or else they'd be poor. In the 1914 short story "Clay," written by James Joyce, the game plays a significant role.

Typically a cake, barmbrack, cranachan, champ, or colcannon, items would be hidden in food in Ireland and Scotland, and portions of the food would be distributed at random. The thing a person found would tell them about their future; For instance, a coin represented wealth, and a ring represented marriage. Halloween bonfires were also used for divination in parts of Brittany, Wales, and Scotland up until the 19th century. A ring of stones, one for each person, would be buried in the ashes after the fire had subsided. If a stone was misplaced in the morning, it was believed that the person it represented would not survive the year.

Halloween parties frequently include activities like telling ghost stories, listening to Halloween-themed music, and watching scary movies. Halloween-themed specials and episodes of television shows usually air on or before Halloween. New horror movies often come out before Halloween to capitalize on the holiday. The specials are usually geared toward children.

*Haunted Attractions*

These are places to have fun and be scared. The majority of attractions are seasonal Halloween businesses that may include hayrides, corn mazes, haunted houses, and other attractions. As the industry has grown, so have the effects' levels of sophistication.

The Orton and Spooner Ghost House, which opened in 1915 in Liphook, England, was the first purpose-built haunted attraction ever documented. In fact, this attraction is most like a steam-powered carnival funhouse. The Hollycombe Steam Collection still contains the House. Haunted houses with Halloween themes first appeared in the United States in the 1930s, roughly at the same time as trick-or-treating. Haunted houses became a popular tourist attraction toward the end of the 1950s, initially in California. The San Mateo Haunted House opened in 1957 under the sponsorship of the Children's Health Home Junior Auxiliary. In 1958, the Haunted House of the San Bernardino Assistance League opened. Between 1962 and 1963, the nation saw the emergence of home haunts. The Children's Museum Haunted House in Indianapolis and the San Manteo Haunted House both opened in 1964.

The opening of the Haunted Mansion in Disneyland on August 12, 1969, is credited with creating the haunted house as a cultural icon in the United States. In 1973, Knott's Scary Farm debuted as its own Halloween-night attraction at Knott's Berry Farm. One of the first "hell houses" was opened in 1972 by evangelical Christians as an adaptation of these attractions. The Sycamore-Deer Park Jaycees in Clifton, Ohio, created the first non-profit Halloween haunted house in 1970. The Cincinnati, Ohio-based AM radio station WSAI served as a co-sponsor. In 1982, it was last produced. After the Ohio house's success, other Jaycees created their own versions. In 1976, the March of Dimes licensed a "Mini Haunted House for the March of

Dimes," and shortly thereafter, they began conducting haunted houses to raise funds through their local chapters. Some March of Dimes haunted houses continue to operate to this day, although it appears that they stopped funding this kind of event on a national scale sometime in the 1980s.

The Haunted Castle (Six Flags Great Adventure) caught fire in Jackson Township, New Jersey, on May 11, 1984, in the late evening. Eight teens lost their lives in the fire. In response to the tragedy, safety regulations, building codes, and the frequency with which attractions are inspected nationwide were tightened. The better-funded commercial businesses stepped in to fill the void left by the inability of the smaller venues, particularly nonprofit attractions, to compete financially. The stricter regulations that are required of permanent attractions now apply to facilities that were previously exempt from regulation because they were regarded as temporary installations.

Theme parks seriously entered the market in the late 1980s and early 1990s. Halloween Horror Nights at Universal Studios Florida began in 1991, and Six Flags Fright Fest began in 1986. In the 1990s, America's obsession with Halloween as a cultural event caused a spike in attendance at Knott's Scary Farm. The holiday has become increasingly global thanks to theme parks. Disney now hosts Mickey's Not-So-Scary Halloween Party events at its parks in Paris, Hong Kong, and Tokyo, as well as in the United States. Both Universal Studios Singapore and Universal Studios Japan participate. In terms of both size and attendance, the haunts at theme parks are by far the largest.

*Food*
A variety of vegetarian dishes are associated with All Hallows' Eve because many Western Christian denominations encourage meat-free

holidays. Candy apples (also known as toffee apples outside of North America), caramel apples, or taffy apples are common Halloween treats that are made by rolling whole apples in a sticky sugar syrup, sometimes followed by rolling them in nuts. In the Northern Hemisphere, Halloween occurs after the annual apple harvest.

Candy apples were once frequently distributed to children participating in trick-or-treating, but the practice quickly declined as a result of widespread rumors that some individuals were encasing items such as pins and razor blades in the apples in the United States. Even though these kinds of incidents have been reported, there is evidence of them, but actual cases of malicious behavior are extremely rare and have never caused serious harm. Nevertheless, a lot of parents believed that the media was to blame for such aberrant behaviors. During the height of the hysteria, some hospitals offered children's Halloween costumes free X-rays to look for signs of tampering. Parents who poisoned their own children's candy made up almost all of the known cases of candy poisoning. The baking of a barmbrack (Irish: ), or more frequently, the purchase of one, is one tradition that still exists in contemporary Ireland. Before baking, a plain ring, a coin, and other charms are inserted into báirn break, a light fruitcake. Being the fortunate person who finds it is considered fortunate. Additionally, it has been asserted that those who acquire a ring will find their true love within the following year. This is similar to the Epiphany celebration custom of king cake.

A list of Halloween-related foods:
Barmbrack (Ireland) Bonfire toffee (Great Britain) Candy apples (Great Britain and Ireland) Candy corn (North America) Candy pumpkins (Ireland and Scotland) Chocolate monkey nuts (peanuts in their shells) Caramel apples Caramel corn Colcannon (Ireland) Halloween cake

Sweets/candy Novelty candy in the shapes of bats, worms, skulls, pumpkins, and so on.

The Vigil of All Hallows is being held at an Episcopal Christian church on Hallowe'en. On Hallowe'en (All Hallows' Eve), believers in Poland were once instructed to pray out loud as they walk through the forests so that the souls of the dead could find comfort. Sweet corn and roasted pumpkin seeds Soul cakes Pumpkin PieOn All Hallows' Eve, Christian priests in small Spanish villages ring their church bells to remind their congregations to remember the dead. Christian abstinence, including serving pancakes or colcannon instead of meat on All Hallows' Eve and among immigrants in Canada, is a tradition in Ireland. Children (angelitos) in Mexico construct an altar to entice the reincarnation of deceased children.

Hallowe'en is traditionally observed by the Christian Church with a vigil. Through prayers and fasting, worshipers prepared for the feast on the following All Saints' Day. The Vigil of All Saints or the Vigil of All Hallows is the name of this church service; Night of Light is a project that aims to spread the Vigil of All Hallows throughout Christendom." suitable festivities and entertainments" and a trip to the cemetery or graveyard, where flowers and candles are often placed in preparation for All Hallows' Day, are common after the service."Are known as valomeri, or seas of light" in Finland because so many people visit the cemeteries on All Hallows' Eve to light votive candles there.

There is a wide range of Christian attitudes toward Halloween today. Some dioceses in the Anglican Church have decided to emphasize the Christian customs associated with All Hallows' Eve. Praying, fasting, and attending worship services are some of these practices. We beseech thee, O LORD, our God, to multiply the blessings of your grace upon us:that those of us who hinder the glorious celebration of your saints may be able to joyfully follow them in all godly behavior. Through Jesus Christ, our Lord, who reigns with you in the unity of the Holy Spirit and is the only God throughout all time. Amen. —Collect of the Vigil of All Saints, The Anglican Breviary Other Protestant Christians observe All Hallows' Eve as Reformation Day to commemorate the Protestant Reformation, either concurrently with All Hallows' Eve or separately from it. This is due to the legend that Martin Luther nailed his Ninety-Five Theses to Wittenberg's All Saints' Church on All Hallows' Eve. On All Hallows' Eve, children participate in "Harvest Festivals" or "Reformation Festivals" by dressing up as Bible characters or Reformers. When children go trick-or-treating on Halloween, many Christians also give them gospel tracts in addition to candy. The American Tract Society claimed that they alone receive orders for approximately 3 million gospel tracts for Halloween celebrations. Others order Scripture Candy with a Halloween theme to distribute to children on this day.

Children in Belize dressed as Christian saints and Biblical figures. Some Christians are concerned about the modern Halloween celebration because they believe it trivializes or celebrates paganism, the occult, or other practices and cultural phenomena that they believe are incompatible with their beliefs." If English and American children like to dress up as witches and devils on one night of the year that is not a problem," said exorcist Father Gabriele Amorth in Rome. There is no harm in playing just a game."The Roman Catholic Archdiocese of Boston has recently celebrated Halloween with a "Saint Fest."In a similar vein, a lot of contemporary Protestant churches see Halloween as a fun holiday for kids, hosting parties where kids and their parents can dress up, play games, and get free candy. Halloween poses no threat to children's spiritual lives for these Christians:Teaching about death and mortality as well as the practices of their Celtic ancestors actually serves as a valuable life lesson and is a part of the heritage of many of their parishioners. Halloween is about "using humor and ridicule to confront the power of death," according to Christian minister Sam Portaro.

Halloween is recognized as having a Christian connection in the Roman Catholic Church, and numerous Catholic parochial schools in the United States hold Halloween celebrations on a regular basis. To capitalize on Halloween's popularity as an opportunity for evangelism, numerous fundamentalist and evangelical churches utilize "Hell houses" and comic-style tracts. Due to its alleged roots in the Festival of the Dead, some people believe that Halloween is incompatible with Christianity. Even though Eastern Orthodox Christians observe All Hallows' Day on the First Sunday after Pentecost, the Eastern Orthodox Church advises that Vespers or a Paraklesis be observed on Western All Hallows' Eve out of a pastoral need to offer a different celebration than popular ones.

*Analogous Celebrations and Perspectives*
**Judaism**
According to Alfred J. Kolatch in the Second Jewish Book of Why, Halloween is against Jewish Halakha because it violates Leviticus 18:3, which prohibits Jews from participating in gentile customs. Yizkor, which is observed communally by many Jews four times a year, is somewhat analogous to Allhallowtide in Christianity in that prayers are said for both "martyrs and one's own family."Despite this, many Jews in the United States observe Halloween without any connection to the Christian holiday. While Reform Rabbi Jeffrey Goldwasser said that "there is no religious reason why contemporary Jews should not celebrate Halloween," Orthodox Rabbi Michael Broyde opposed Jews celebrating Halloween.

## Islam

A Brief Illustrated Guide to Understanding Islam by Sheikh Idris Palmer has decreed that Muslims should not celebrate Halloween because it is "worse than participating in Christmas, Easter,... it is more sinful than congratulating the Christians for their prostration to the crucifix." According to the National Fatwa Council of Malaysia, "Halloween is celebrated using a humorous theme mixed with horror to entertain and resist the spirit of death that influences humans," it has also been ruled to be haram due to its alleged pagan roots. Dar Al-Ifta Al-Misriyya disagrees, provided that the celebration is not referred to as an "eid" and that the behavior adheres to Islamic norms.

## Hinduism

During the festival of Pitru Paksha, when Hindus pay homage to and perform a ceremony "to keep the souls of their ancestors at rest," Hindus remember the deceased. It is observed during the Hindu month of Bhadrapada, which falls around the middle of September. Some Hindus choose to observe Halloween's well-known traditions even though the Hindu festival of Diwali sometimes falls on Halloween. Other Hindus, like Soumya Dasgupta, have opposed the holiday because "our indigenous festivals" have been negatively impacted by Western holidays like Halloween.

## Neopaganism

Those who identify as Neo-Pagans or Wiccans do not adhere to a single standard or viewpoint regarding Halloween. Some Neopagans observe Samhain instead, which takes place on November 1. However, others enjoy the Halloween celebrations, claiming that one can observe both "the solemnity of Samhain and the fun of Halloween."According to some neopagans, the celebration of Halloween trivializes Samhain and should be avoided because of the interruptions caused by trick-or-treaters."Wiccans don't officially celebrate Halloween, even though the 31st of October will still have a star beside it in any good Wiccan's day planner," the Manitoban writes. Samhain is a holiday celebrated by Wiccans that begins at sunset. Samhain is a Celtic festival that is not restricted to Neopagan religions like Wicca. Modern Wiccans do not attempt to imitate Samhain celebrations, although these customs originated in Celtic nations. Even though some of the old Samhain rituals are still done, the main point is that Samhain is a time to celebrate the dead and darkness. This may be why people often mistake Samhain for Halloween.

*Geography of Halloween*

The significance and customs of Halloween vary greatly from country to country. Children dressed in costumes go "guising" and have parties in Scotland and Ireland for Halloween. In Ireland, other Halloween traditions include lighting bonfires and displaying fireworks. Children in Brittany would make fun of visitors to graveyards by lighting candles inside skulls to scare them. Halloween's widespread transatlantic immigration in the 19th century made it popular in North America. The way Halloween is celebrated in the United States and Canada has had a significant impact on how it is celebrated elsewhere. Ecuador, Chile, Australia, New Zealand, the majority of continental Europe, Finland, Japan, and other parts of East Asia have all experienced this larger North American influence, particularly in terms of commercial and iconic elements.

Chapter 3

# FACTS ABOUT HALLOWEEN

25 Interesting Halloween Facts
Over the centuries, the spooky holiday has grown from a religious holiday to one of the most commercialized holidays of the year.
If you're a trivia champion who wants to learn more about the seasons, you've come to the right place. How knowledgeable are you on Halloween? It doesn't matter if you already have your costume picked out, your Halloween treats and candy are hidden away so you can't eat them all before the big night, and your scary movie is ready to watch.

1 . The holiday has been observed for more than 2,000 years. Halloween has been around longer than Christianity. Samhain, which translates to "summer's end," was the pre-Christian Celtic festival that gave rise to all of this. The feast, which was held around the first of November, celebrated the last day of the fall harvest and the crossing of spirits because it was believed that the veil between the living and the spirit worlds became thinner on that day. In the past, people in Northern France, the United Kingdom, and Ireland burned sacrificed bonfires and, yes, donned costumes to deceive the spirits to ward off ghosts.

2 . Since the Middle Ages, trick-or-treating has been practiced. stealing candy from strangers just one night a year is not a new custom. In Scotland and Ireland at the time, it was referred to as "guising."Young people donned costumes and went door to door in search of food or cash in exchange for performing songs, poems, or other "tricks."Today, the custom has evolved into children dressing up

and requesting candy. Nowadays, very few people do anything for their candy, but a simple "thank you" can go a long way.

3. Historically, finding a husband was one of the Halloween rituals. Halloween customs were created by single women in the 18th century to assist them in finding romantic partners.History.com says that women used to throw apple peels over their shoulders in the hope that when they landed, they would see their future husband's initials in the pattern. They were supposed to marry first if they bobbed for apples at parties. They even used to stand in a dark room with a candle in their hands in front of a mirror to see if their future husband's face would show up in the reflection.

4. The Irish brought their Halloween customs with them when they fled their country's potato famine in the 1840s, helping to spread the holiday throughout the United States. Halloween pranksters reached an all-time high in the 1920s when the celebration spread across the nation. Community-based trick-or-treating, according to some, became popular in the 1930s as a way to rein in overindulgent pranksters.

5. Trick-or-treating was halted during World War II due to sugar rationing. During World War II, trick-or-treating was less popular due to a lack of sweet treats. All systems started collecting candy after the rationing ended. To capitalize on the tradition and ensure that children were clamoring for their products to appear in their candy buckets and spare pillowcases, candy companies began launching advertising campaigns.

6. Halloween is now the nation's second-largest commercial holiday. It only comes second after Christmas. The National Retail Federation estimates that in 2019, consumers spent approximately $9 billion

celebrating Halloween. Despite a slight dip in spending in 2020 due to the COVID-19 pandemic, Americans still spent over $8 billion, or $92 per person, overall.

7. The majority of Americans spend money on costumes, candy, and decorations.
When it comes to our love of Halloween, many of us put our money where our mouths are.95% of people plan to buy candy, 75% plan to buy decorations, and 65% plan to buy costumes. The majority of people also plan to buy costumes. If you're wondering why we all tighten our belts (and our wallets) in January, Americans spent an average of $1,048 on winter holidays in 2019.

8. An Irish legend inspired jack-o-lanterns.
According to the legend, the origin of the term "jack-o'-lantern" comes from an Irish folktale about a man named "Stingy Jack" who deceived the devil and was forced to walk the Earth with only coal burning in a hollow turnip to guide him. He was first referred to as "Jack o'Lantern" by the Irish, then as "Jack of the Lantern."

9. They were previously prepared with turnips, potatoes, and beets.
After all, jack-o-lanterns did originate in Ireland. Pumpkins were used in place of candy when Halloween became popular in the United States. For a more natural look that also has historical roots, you might want to consider adding some creative products to your Halloween tableau this year. They also make an excellent side dish for dinner after the holiday is over!

10. In addition, traditional Halloween bread is produced in Ireland.
It is known as barmbrack, or simply "brack."A small hidden toy or ring, in addition to dark and golden raisins, is typically included in the sweet loaf. The item is believed to bring good fortune to the person who finds

it, just like the traditional king cake at Mardi Gras. That is, as long as the trinket does not cause them to choke.

11. Disney was close to making Hocus Pocus a different movie.
The Halloween favorite that everyone loves almost didn't become what it is today. The script for the original title, Disney's Halloween House, was significantly scarier and darker. Additionally, Leonardo DiCaprio was offered the role of Max Dennison, a teen love interest, but he declined the role to appear in What's Eating Gilbert Grape instead.

12. Up to five times more pumpkins are produced in Illinois than in any other state.
If you're looking for a truly memorable pumpkin patch, head to the heartland. The gourd industry occupies more than 15,000 acres in the Land of Lincoln, according to the US Department of Agriculture. Over 500 million pounds of pumpkins are typically produced annually on these Illinois farms.

13. "Chicken feed" was the original name for candy corn.
To appeal to America's agricultural roots, the Goelitz Confectionery Company initially sold the controversial treat in boxes featuring a rooster on the front. Since the 1880s, the sugary recipe has largely remained unchanged. You can't argue with that level of consistency, whether you like them or not.

14. "Billboard's charts once belonged to "Monster Mash."
In 1962, just before Halloween, Bobby "Boris" Pickett reached the top of the Hot 100, and in 1973, in August, he made it back to the top spot. It could even be described as "a graveyard smash!"

15. Hawaii even has a pumpkin patch that you can visit.
Pick pumpkins on Oahu at Waimanalo Country Farms, whether you live there or just want a taste of home while you're on vacation. In search of squash in Florida? Try Dunnellon's, Pickin' Patch. The rest of the year, it's a watermelon farm, but during the fall and winter, it focuses on pumpkins.

16. The story behind Halloween's Michael Myers mask is fascinating. The well-known antagonist from horror films comes from a surprisingly innocent upbringing. Production designer Tommy Lee Wallace purchased two masks from a magic shop on Hollywood Boulevard while working on the original 1978 film:a clown mask and William Shatner, who plays Captain Kirk in the Star Trek series.
"When Tommy entered wearing the clown mask, we thought, "Ooh, that's kind of scary." We stopped dead and said, 'It's perfect,'" actor Nick Castle told the New York Times after he donned the Shatner mask. They gave it a white spray paint finish, made the eye holes bigger, and the rest is history.

17. Carving the fastest pumpkin took just 16.47 seconds.
Stephen Clarke of New York is the person who carved the fastest lantern in the Guinness Book of World Records in October 2013. The jack-o-lantern had to have an entire face, including eyes, nose, mouth, and ears, to win the prize. Whether the expression was funny or scary is unknown.

18. The largest Halloween parade in the United States is held in New York City each year, attracting over 2 million spectators and thousands of participants along the route. Ralph Lee, a Greenwich Village resident, and puppeteer came up with the idea to just throw a fun walk from house to house for his kids and their friends. When a nearby theater heard about it, they joined in and made the event bigger. Every

year since it has grown in size, and become more imaginative and become more theatrical.

19. The most popular costumes for kids are those featuring superheroes and princesses.
The National Retail Federation says that adults most often dress as witches. Pumpkin costumes were the most popular for dogs in 2019, Cats' most common costume is to hide under the couch and hiss at the thought.

20. The best candy for Halloween is Skittles.
Why no chocolate?No issue! CandyStore's 11-year sales history shows that the fruit candies in bite-sized packages outsold M&Ms, Snickers, and Reese's Cups. According to a survey conducted by CandyStore, even though candy corn made the top 10, the tricolored treats also ranked among the worst Halloween candies. It's no wonder candy trades on Halloween night get so heated.

21. Teens over 16 were prohibited from trick-or-treating in a Canadian city. News reports claim that anyone over the age of 16 who is caught trick-or-treating in Bathurst, Canada, faces a fine of up to $200.Everyone in the city has a curfew, so no one under 16 can go out after 8 p.m. on Halloween. After a rash of pranks, the rules were enacted to curb after-dark mischief.

22. In 1926, Harry Houdini passed away on Halloween.
On October 31, the well-known entertainer, illusionist, and magician passed away from peritonitis brought on by a ruptured appendix. However, as would be expected of a man of mystery, numerous contradictory reports emerged at the time. Some say he was poisoned by a group of irate Spiritualists, while others say his appendix burst when a student punched him in the stomach (with his permission).On

the evening of October 24, 1926, he performed and was rushed to the hospital in Detroit, Michigan. A week later, he passed away from peritonitis, or organ inflammation brought on by organ leakage.

23. Black cat adoptions were previously suspended for Halloween at some shelters.
In the days leading up to Halloween, they were concerned that the animals were in danger from satanic cults that wanted them for evil purposes. But shelters are now moving in the opposite direction. Using the pre-adoption screening and interview process to eliminate anyone with ill will, many even promote black cat adoptions in October.

24. The number of jack-o-lanterns displayed holds the record for Keene, New Hampshire.
With 30,581 lit pumpkins scattered throughout the city in October 2013, the city surpassed the previous record. Keene set the previous record in this category and has since broken it eight times. Talk about making the night shine!

25. In some places, Mischief Night or Goosey Night is the night before Halloween.
If you've ever lived on the East Coast or in the Midwest, you probably already know that on October 30 a lot of teens and tweens pull pranks. The custom, on the other hand, never really made it to the West Coast, where it was practiced in a variety of ways, including egging cars and other riskier pranks like putting toilet paper on trees outside of homes. The majority of people celebrate the holiday in Pennsylvania, New Jersey, and Michigan, where it is known as Devil's Night and Mischief Night, respectively.

## 15 Halloween Trivia To Test Your Spooky Knowledge!

What is the spooky season, exactly? Some might refer to it as Halloween, All Saints' Day, or All Hallows Eve. Regardless, October 31 is known by a variety of names and is unquestionably one of our nation's most beloved holidays. However, even though you've probably been celebrating Halloween all of your life, there may still be a lot you don't know about it. We've compiled some fun Halloween facts below to help you refresh your trivia knowledge.

1. The Old English word wicce, which means "wise woman," is the origin of the word "witch." Taking things one step further, "wiccans" were actually regarded favorably and respected for their viewpoints. This most likely might have been helpful in Salem...

2. There is a reason why Halloween is associated with orange and black. Black is a symbol of darkness and serves as a reminder that Halloween was once a festival that marked the boundaries between life and death, while orange represents the harvest of autumn.

3. The holiday's earliest agricultural roots are represented by scarecrows. That is correct! In order to safeguard their crops, Greek farmers developed the first scarecrows that resemble people. The name came from the fact that crows were the main problem.

4. Pumpkins are not considered a vegetable but rather fruit.
A fruit is basically anything that grows from something like a flower.

5. Originally, Halloween was a Celtic holiday.
According to the History Channel, the ancient Celtic festival of Samhain, which was celebrated on October 31 on the eve of their new year, is where Halloween got its start 2,000 years ago. Since the Celts

believed that the dead would come back to life that night, they made bonfires and dressed in costumes to keep the ghosts away.

6. A custom known as "mumming" was another source of inspiration for trick-or-treating. In the middle ages, people started the practice of mumming, in which they went door to door dressed as ghosts and demons and performed plays and songs in exchange for food and drink. It is believed that this practice predates trick-or-treating.

7. Trick-or-treaters didn't get candy until the 1950s.
Without those amusing (and king!) characters, Halloween simply would not be the same. Size candy bars to help you feel better. However, according to the History Channel, there was a time when trick-or-treaters received pieces of cake, fruit, nuts, coins, and small toys instead of candy. Candy didn't become a staple on the trick-or-treating circuit until the 1950s when candy manufacturers started promoting their products for Halloween. Nowadays, Halloween purchases account for one-quarter of all candy sales in the United States annually.

8. A creepy Halloween costume is still a favorite with everyone.
Despite the fact that cute, funny, or silly costumes are still the most popular Halloween outfits, the National Retail Federation states that the most popular adult Halloween costumes for 2020 were:
1. Witch
2. Vampire
3. Cat
4. Batman
5. Ghost

9. America's favorite candy is Skittles.
On Halloween 2020, everyone wanted to taste the rainbow! Skittles, Reese's Cups, and Starburst were the most popular candy last year, according to CandyStore.

10. America's least favorite candy is candy corn.
Candy corn has always divided people, but CandyStore.com's most recent lists of the 10 worst Halloween candy items show that more people don't like it than they do. In 2019 and 2020, consumers ranked candy corn as the worst Halloween candy in the nation. To be fair, it also made the list of the top 10 best Halloween candies for 2020, suggesting that the debate is not yet over!

11. The fear of Halloween is known as Samhainophobia
The spooky spirit of Halloween is enjoyed by many, but for some, the fear is not always fun. Samhainophobia, or the fear of Halloween, affects some people. After learning about the history of Halloween, you probably already know that the word comes from Samhain, the Gaelic festival that gave Halloween its name.

12. Hollywood prohibits Silly String on Halloween.
According to reports in the media, using Silly String on Halloween can result in a $1,000 fine in Hollywood.

13. The longest haunted house in the world is 3,564 feet long.
In Lewisburg, Ohio, the Haunted Cave is 80 feet underground. Creepy!

14. Halloween House was the original title of Disney's Hocus Pocus.
At first, the popular Halloween movie was supposed to be more scary than funny. Thank goodness that fate intervened.

15. It is the horror film with the greatest commercial success of all time.
Global box office receipts for the 2017 adaptation of Stephen King's classic horror novel reached $700,381,759.

www.ingramcontent.com/pod-product-compliance
Lightning Source LLC
Chambersburg PA
CBHW080953220526

45465CB00008BA/3261